THE VOCAL LIBRARY

LOW VOICE

HYMN CLASSICS

concert arrangements of traditional hymns
for voice and piano

To access companion recorded performances
and piano accompaniments online, visit:
www.halleonard.com/mylibrary

Enter Code
4863-7528-8417-9648

Concert Arrangements by Richard Walters

On the cover: John Ritto Penniman, American 1783-c. 1830, *Meetinghouse Hill, Roxbury, Massachusetts*,
1799, oil on canvas, 29 x 37 in., Centennial Year Acquisition and the Centennial Fund for Major Acquisitions,
1979.1461, © 1993 The Art Institute of Chicago.

ISBN 978-0-7935-6007-3

HAL•LEONARD® CORPORATION

7777 W. BLUEMOUND RD. P.O. BOX 13819 MILWAUKEE, WI 53213

T0050959

Visit Hal Leonard Online at
www.halleonard.com

ON THE RECORDING...

ANNE LARSON, mezzo-soprano, has performed a deep and varied repertoire of opera, oratorio and recital to critical acclaim. Her operatic career has included over 25 roles, including Azucena in *Il Trovatore*, Baba in *The Medium*, and Nancy in Flotow's *Martha*. She has well over 100 performances with Des Moines Metro Opera, having been a principal part of the company since its founding in 1973. Mrs. Larson is a talented teacher of voice, and is on the faculty at Simpson College in Indianola, Iowa. She is deeply devoted to expressing her faith in song.

KIMM JULIAN, baritone, sings major opera roles all over the U.S. He has been heard with many companies, from Washington Opera to Minnesota Opera to Des Moines Metro Opera to Sacramento Opera. Mr. Julian has a huge collection of over 50 roles on stage, including Scarpia, Jack Rance, Rigoletto, Valentin, Tonio, Silvio, Don Giovanni, Germont, the Hoffmann villains, Eugene Onegin, Horace Tabor, and principal roles in *Il Trovatore*, *Un Ballo in Maschera*, *The Crucible*, and *Lucia di Lammermoor*. He made his European debut with the Opera Company of Northern Ireland in Belfast.

CAROL STUART, soprano, was hailed by *The New York Times* as making a "glowing recital debut." Her versatility and dramatic strengths are shown in a career that has included a wide range of 25 leading roles with several opera companies. She was the principal leading soprano with Des Moines Metro Opera for the company's first decade. Ms. Stuart's recital, concert, and oratorio repertoire has included everything from Bach to Barber and beyond. She has a successful private voice studio, and is also on the faculty at Simpson College in Iowa. Ms. Stuart may also be heard on the album "Songs of Joseph Marx."

RICHARD WALTERS, pianist and arranger, is a composer who specializes in writing music for the voice. His principal composition studies were with Dominick Argento. Besides his work as a composer, Mr. Walters is supervising editor of the concert music division at Hal Leonard Corporation, and develops a wide variety of publications in his position. He has great versatility as a musician, working as a classical and popular pianist, a coach for opera and musical theatre, stage director for opera, music critic, author, recording producer, commercial music arranger, orchestrator, and church music director. Walters arrangements may be heard on the Hal Leonard releases "Classical Carols" and "Popular Ballads for Classical Singers."

Contents

On the recording:
* Anne Larson, mezzo-soprano
** Kimm Julian, baritone
*** Carol Stuart, soprano; Anne Larson, mezzo-soprano
Richard Walters, pianist, for all selections

Recorded 5/93 and 7/93, Simpson College, Indianola, Iowa

This collection is happily dedicated to Anne and Carol.

The price of this publication includes access to companion recorded performances and piano accompaniments online, for download or streaming, using the unique code found on the title page.
Visit **www.halleonard.com/mylibrary** and enter the access code.

for Kimm

COME, THOU FOUNT OF EVERY BLESSING

Robert Robinson, 1758

American Folk Tune
First set by John Wyeth, 1813
arranged by Richard Walters

flam - ing tongues a - bove; Praise the _ mount! I'm fixed up - on it, Mount of

Thy re - deem-ing _ love. Here I _

raise mine Eb - en - e - zer, Hith-er _ by Thy Help I'm

come; And I _ hope, _ by Thy good _ pleas - ure, Safe - ly _

to ar - rive at _ home. Je - sus_ sought me when a stran - ger, Wan-der-ing

from the fold of _ God; He, to _ res - cue me from _

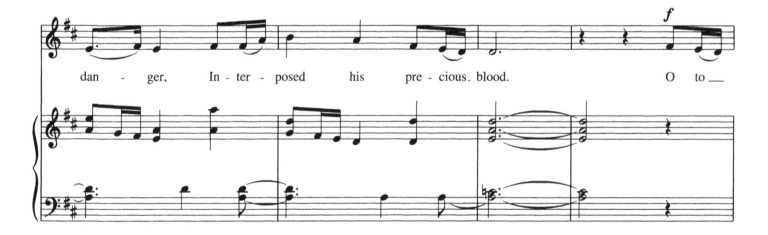

dan - ger, In - ter - posed his pre - cious_ blood. O to _

grace how great a debt - or Dai - ly _ I'm con - strained to

for Gayletha

NOW THANK WE ALL OUR GOD

Martin Rinckart, c. 1636
translated by Catherine Winkworth, 1858

"Nun danket alle Gott"
melody by Johann Crüger, 1648
altered by Felix Mendelssohn, 1840
arranged by Richard Walters

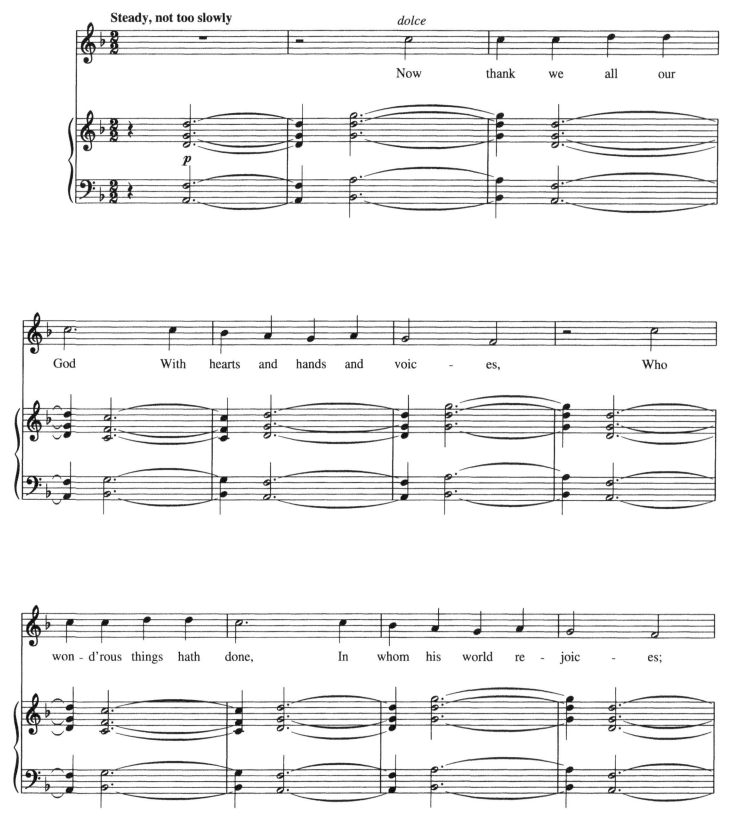

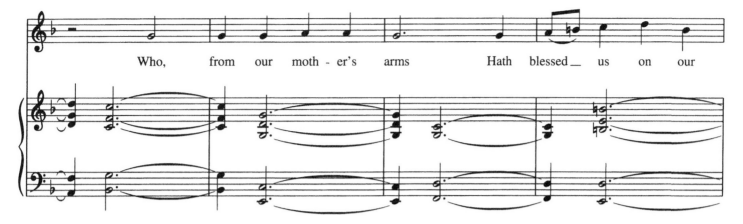

Who, from our moth - er's arms Hath blessed __ us on our

poco rit.

way With count - less gifts of love, And still is ours to -

a tempo

day.

mp espressivo

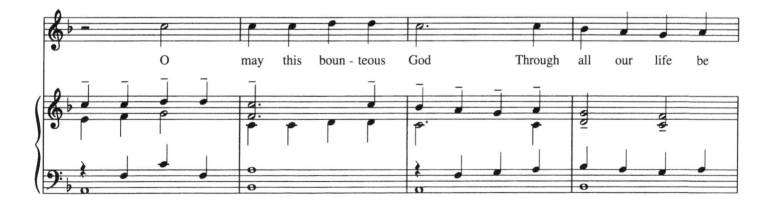

O may this boun - teous God Through all our life be

near   us,   With   ev - er   joy - ful

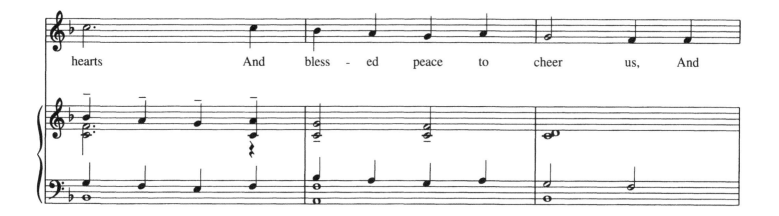

hearts   And   bless - ed   peace   to   cheer   us,   And

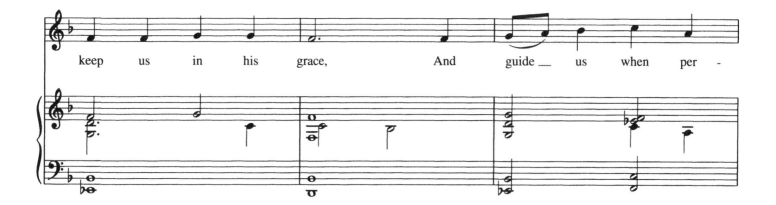

keep   us   in   his   grace,   And   guide __ us   when   per -

plexed,   And   free   us   from   all

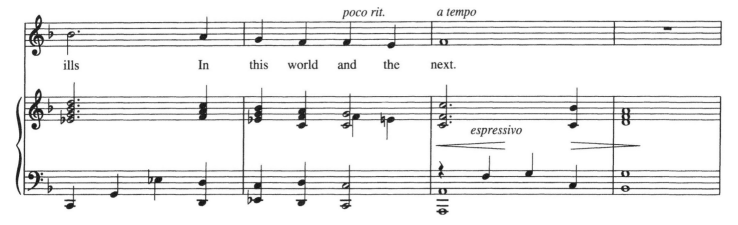

poco rit.　　*a tempo*

ills　　In　this　world　and　the　next.

espressivo

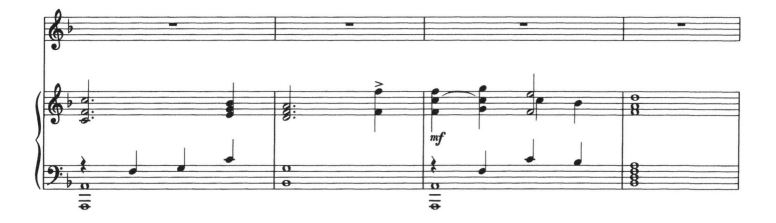

mf

All　praise and thanks to　God　The

f

mf/f

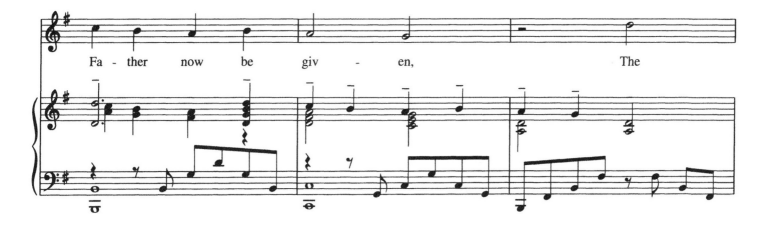

Fa - ther　now　be　giv - en,　The

Son, and him who reigns with them in high-est heav-en,

The one e-ter-nal God, Whom

sub. *p*

cresc. *poco rit.* **More Broadly to the End**

earth __ and heav'n a-dore For

cresc. *poco rit.* *mf* *cresc.* *f*

rit.

thus it was, is now, And shall be __ ev-er more.

rit.

8ba-

for Steve

BE THOU MY VISION

Ancient Irish
translated by Mary E. Byrne, 1905
versified by Eleanor H. Hull, 1912

Traditional Irish Melody
arranged by Richard Walters

Moving along

Be thou my __ vi - sion, O Lord of my

heart, Naught be all else to me save that thou art.

Thou my __ best __ thought, __ by day or by night, _____ Wak - ing or

sleep - ing, thy __ pres - ence, my light _____

mp espressivo

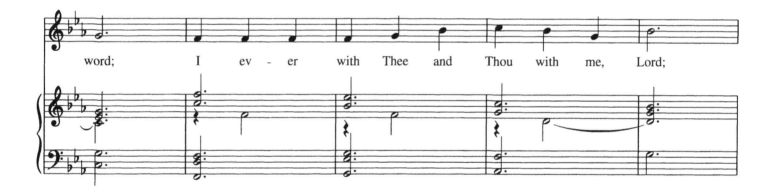

Be Thou my __ wis - dom, and Thou my true

p   *mp*

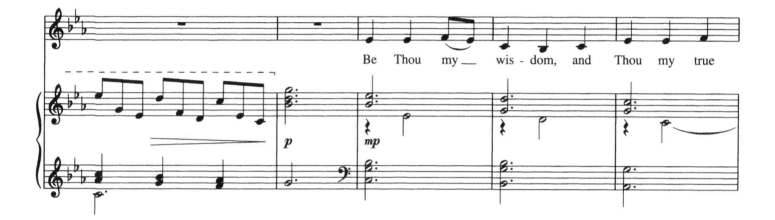

word;   I   ev - er   with   Thee   and   Thou   with   me, Lord;

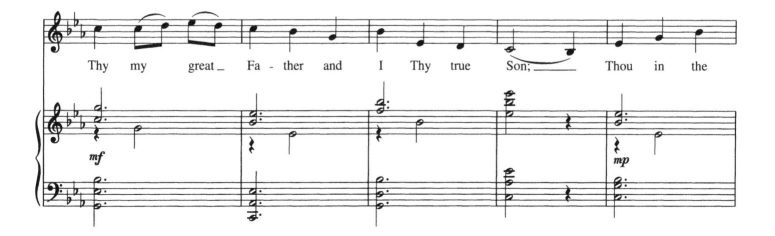

Thy   my   great __ Fa - ther   and   I   Thy   true   Son; _____   Thou   in   the

mf   *mp*

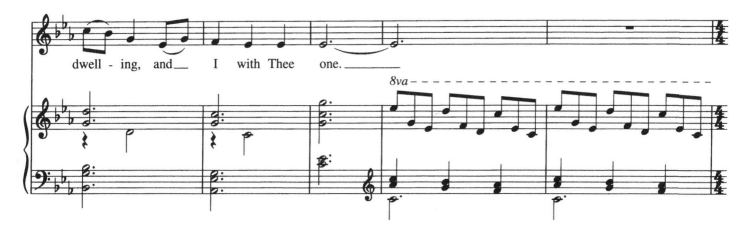

dwell - ing, and__ I with Thee one.__

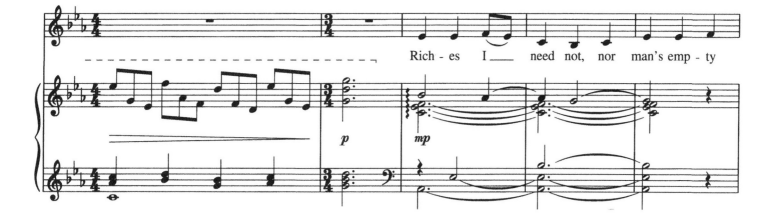

Rich - es I__ need not, nor man's emp - ty

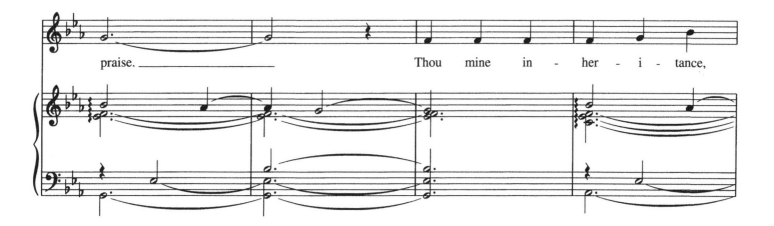

praise.__ Thou mine in - her - i - tance,

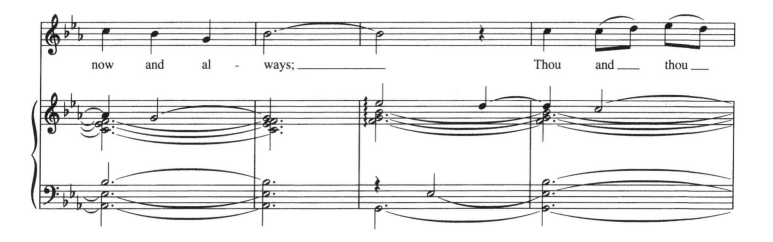

now and al - ways;__ Thou and__ thou__

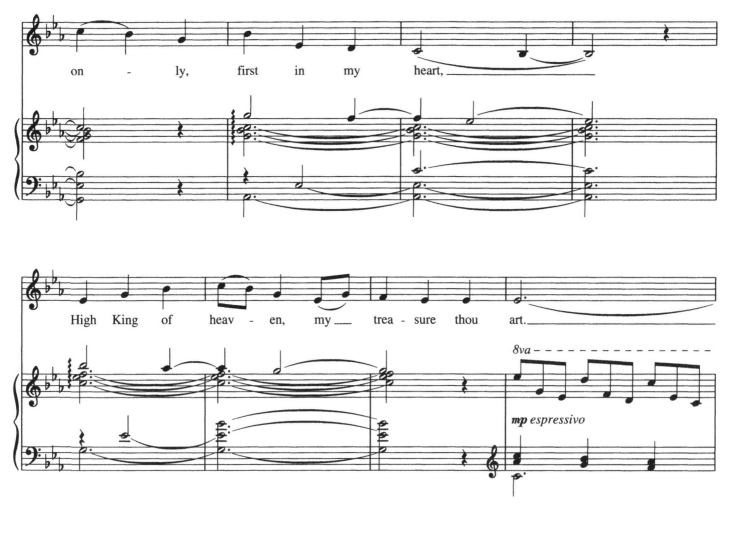

on - ly, first in my heart, _____

High King of heav - en, my ___ trea - sure thou art. _____

mp espressivo

8va - - - - - - - - - - -

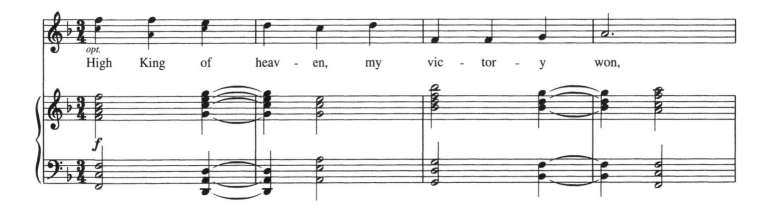

High King of heav - en, my vic - tor - y won,

opt.

f

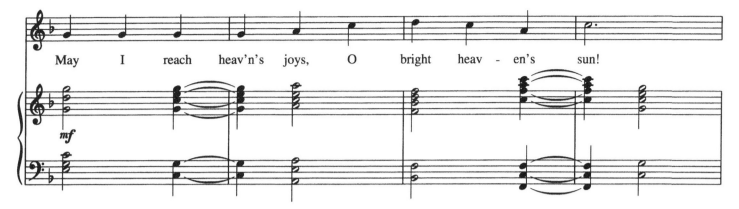

May I reach heav'n's joys, O bright heav-en's sun!

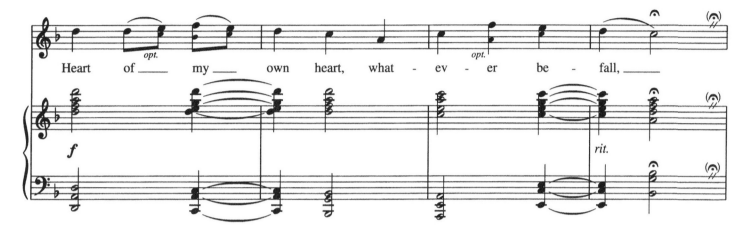

Heart of ___ my ___ own heart, what - ev - er be - fall, ___

Still be my vi - sion, O ru - ler of all. ___

* From here to the end may be either *piano* or *forte,* depending on the singer's best attributes.

for Ida

PRAISE TO THE LORD, THE ALMIGHTY

after Psalm 103
Joachim Neander, 1680
translated by Catherine Winkworth and others

"Lobe den Herren"
Ernewerten Gesangbuch, Stralsund, 1665
arranged by Richard Walters

Brightly, in 1

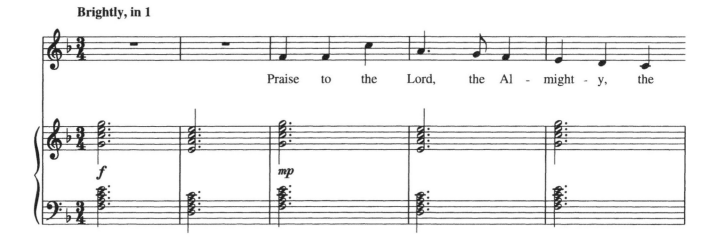

Praise to the Lord, the Al - might - y, the

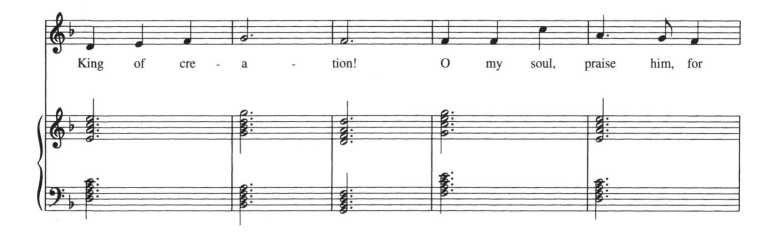

King of cre - a - tion! O my soul, praise him, for

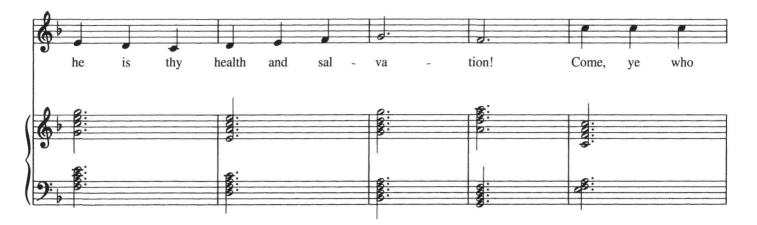

he is thy health and sal - va - tion! Come, ye who

hear, Bro - thers and sis - ters draw near, Praise him in

glad ad - o - ra - tion!

Praise to the Lord, who o'er

all things so won - d'rous - ly reign - eth,

Shel - ters thee un - der his wings, yea, so gent - ly sus -

tain - eth! Hast thous not seen

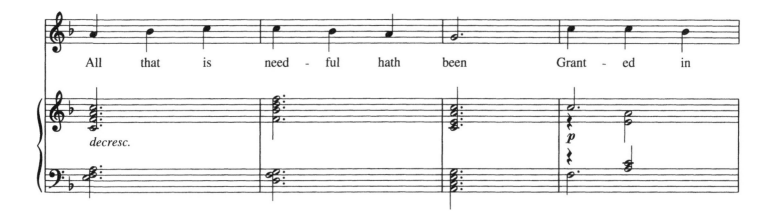

All that is need - ful hath been Grant - ed in

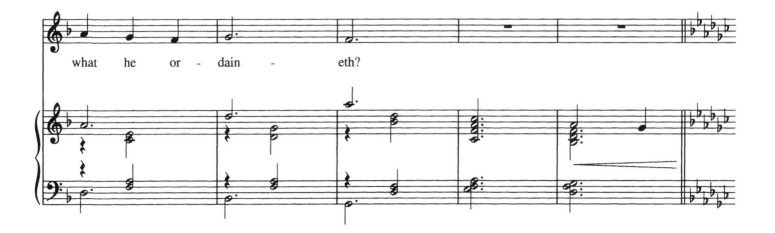

what he or - dain - eth?

Praise to the Lord, who doth pros - per thy work and de -

fend thee; Sure - ly his good - ness and

mer - cy here dai - ly at - tend thee.

Pon - der a - new All the Al - might - y can

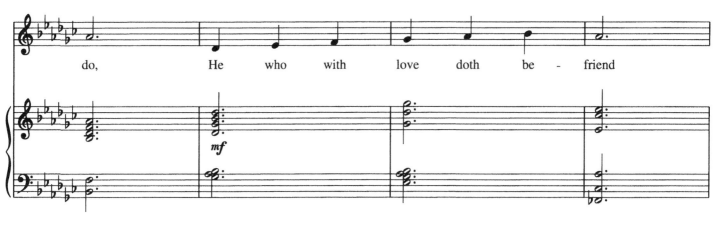

do, He who with love doth be - friend thee.

mf

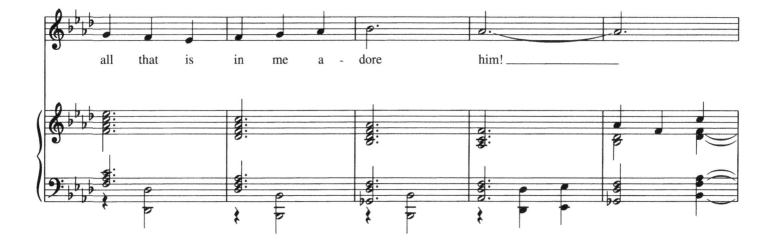

thee. Praise to the Lord! O let

f

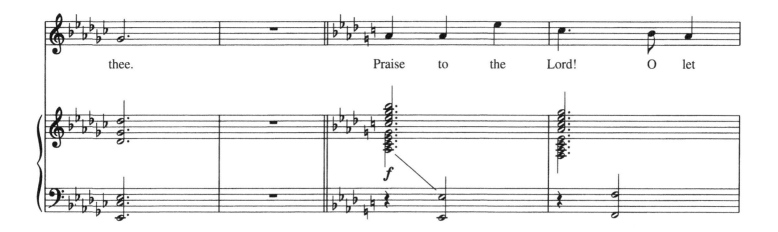

all that is in me a - dore him! _____

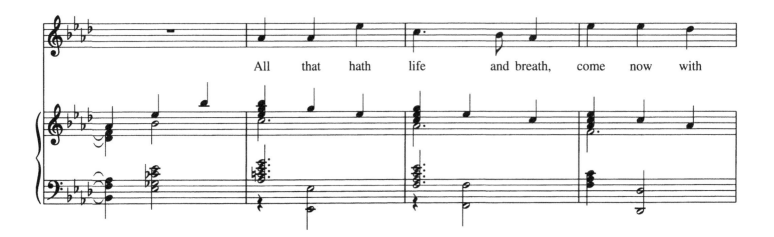

All that hath life and breath, come now with

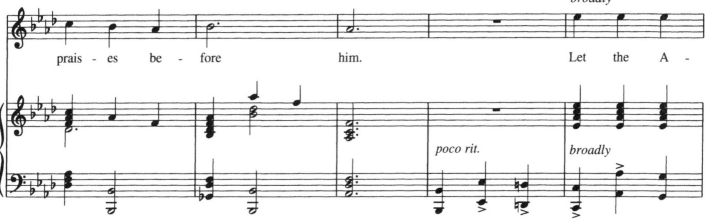

praises be - fore him. Let the A -

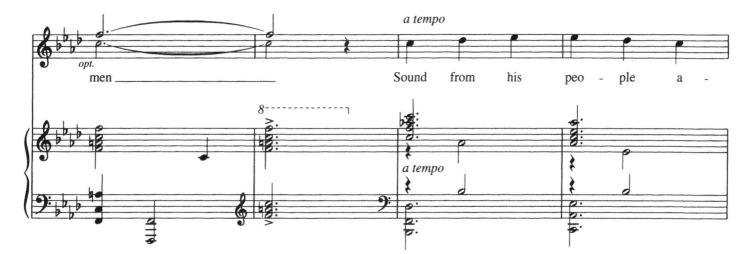

men ____ Sound from his peo - ple a -

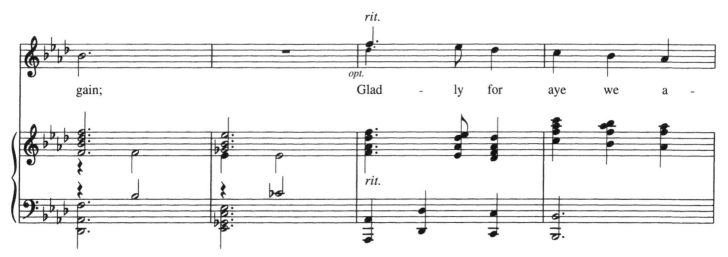

gain; Glad - ly for aye we a -

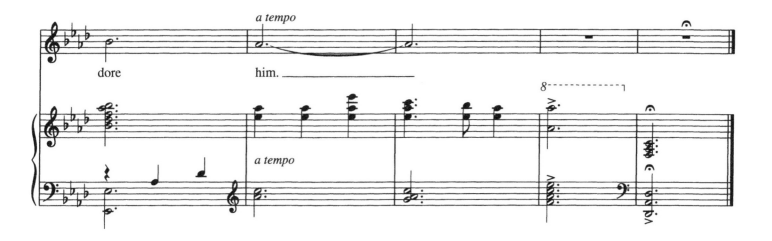

dore him. ____

for Sharon

AH, HOLY JESUS

Johann Heermann, 1630
translated by Robert S. Bridges, 1899

"Herzliebster Jesu"
Johann Crüger, 1640
arranged by Richard Walters

Steady, expressive

O most af - flict - ed! Who was the guil - ty? Who brought this up - on thee? A - las, my trea - son, Je - sus, hath un - done thee! 'Twas I, Lord Je - sus, I it was de - nied thee, I cru - ci - fied thee.

espressivo

mp

mf

mp

espressivo

mf

For me, kind Je - sus,

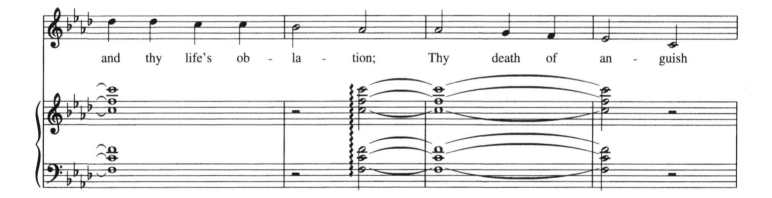

was thy in - car - na - tion, Thy mor - tal sor - row,

and thy life's ob - la - tion; Thy death of an - guish

dolce, rit.

and thy bit - ter pas - sion, For my sal - va - tion.

rit.

espressivo

Slower

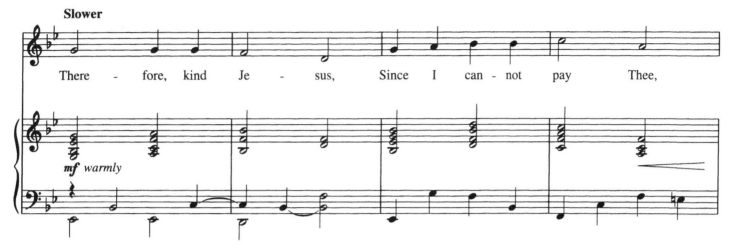

There - fore, kind Je - sus, Since I can - not pay Thee,

mf warmly

I do a - dore Thee, and will ev - er pray thee,

cresc.   *f*

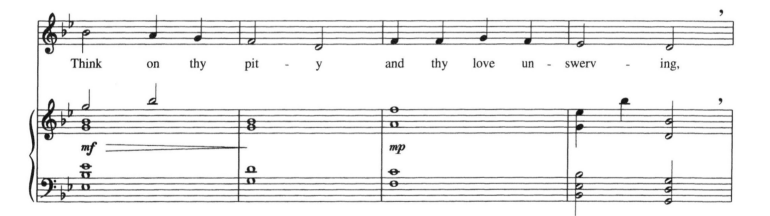

Think on thy pit - y and thy love un - swerv - ing,

mf   *mp*

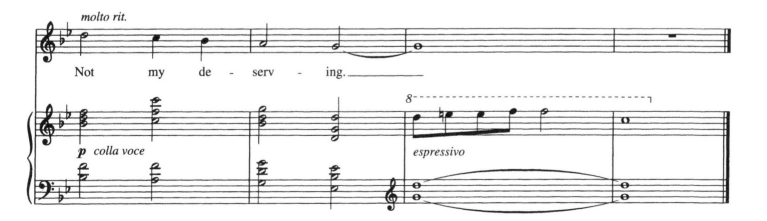

molto rit.

Not my de - serv - ing.

p colla voce   *espressivo*

for Betsy and Harvey

O FOR A THOUSAND TONGUES TO SING

Charles Wesley, 1739 (later altered)

Carl G. Gläser, 1784-1839
Mason's *Modern Psalmody,* 1839
arranged by Richard Walters

O for a thou-sand tongues to sing My great Re-deem-er's praise, The glo-ries of my God and King, The __ tri-umphs of his grace.

My gra-cious Mas - ter and my God, As - sist me to pro - claim, To spread thru all the earth a - broad The hon - ors of thy name.

A little slower

To God all glo - ry, praise and love Be now and ev - er

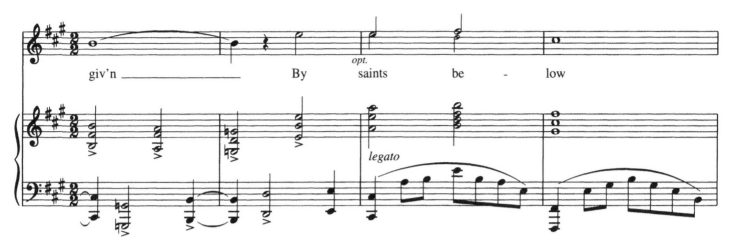

giv'n _____ By saints be - low

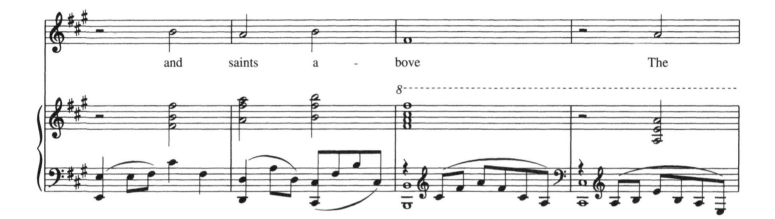

and saints a - bove The

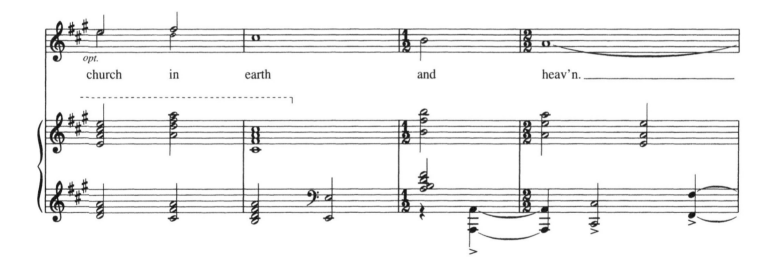

church in earth and heav'n. _____

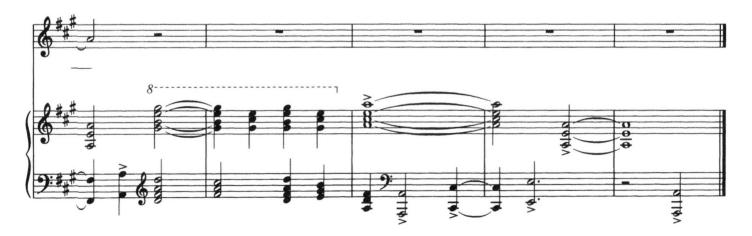

for Russ and Rose Marie

HOW FIRM A FOUNDATION

John Rippon's *A Selection of Hymns,* 1787

Early American Melody
arranged by Richard Walters

ex - cel - lent word! What more can he say than to

you he hath said, To _____ you who for ref - uge to

Je - sus have fled?

Fear ___ not I am with thee, oh be not dis - mayed, For ___ I am thy God and will still give thee aid. I'll strength - en thee, help thee, and cause thee to stand, Up - held by my right - eous om -

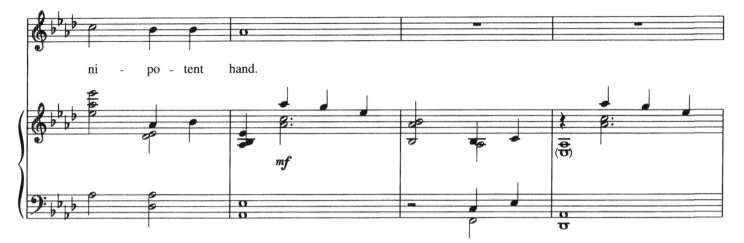

ni - po - tent hand.

mf

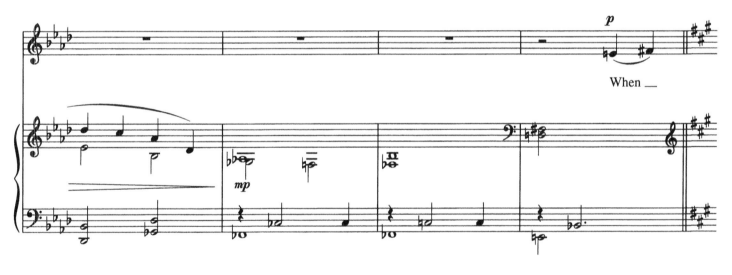

p cresc.

mf

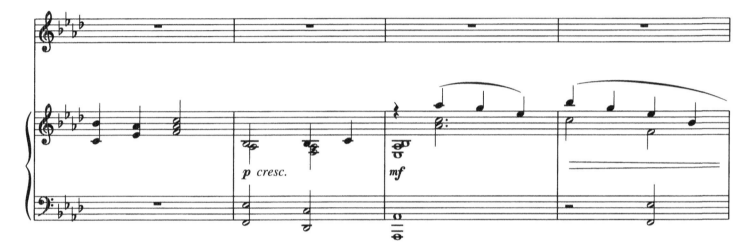

mp

p

When __

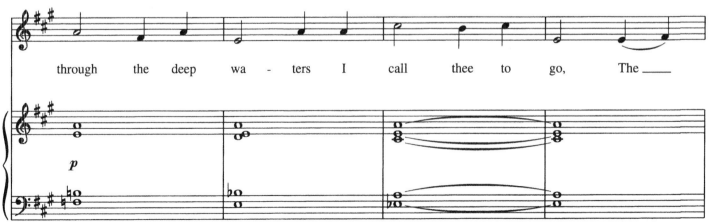

through the deep wa - ters I call thee to go, The ____

p

rivers of woe shall not thee o - ver - flow; For

I will be near thee, thy trou - bles to bless, And ____

sanc - ti - fy to thee thy deep - est dis - tress.

mp

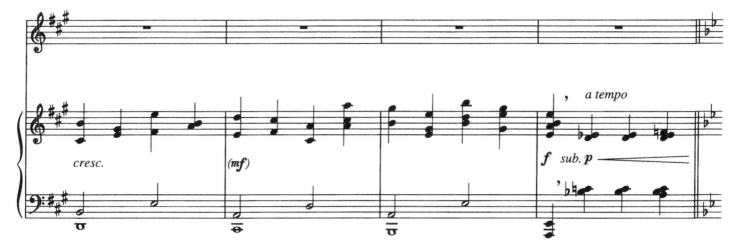

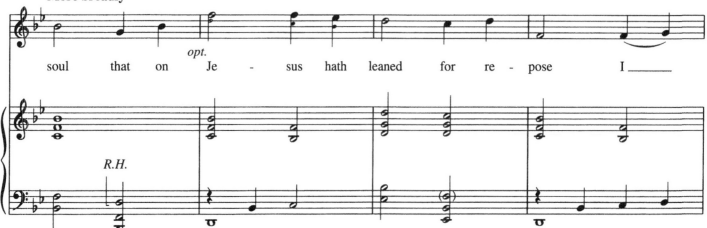

More broadly

soul that on Je - sus hath leaned for re - pose I ____

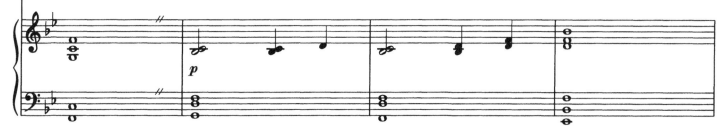

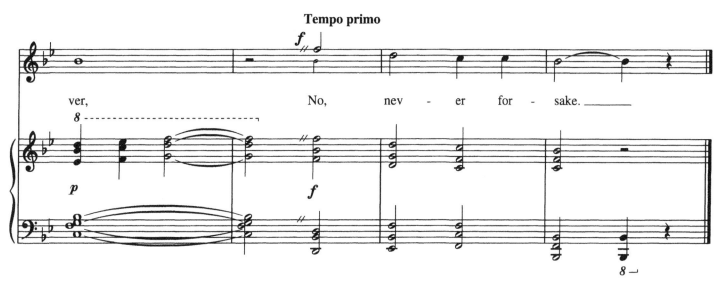

will not, I will not des - sert to his foes,

That soul, though all hell ____ should en - deav - or to

shake, I'll ____ nev - er, no ne -

ver, No, nev - er for - sake. ____

for Robert

LET US BREAK BREAD TOGETHER

African–American Spiritual
arranged by Richard Walters

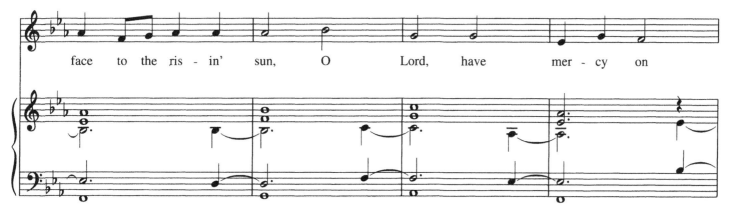

face to the ris - in' sun, O Lord, have mer - cy on

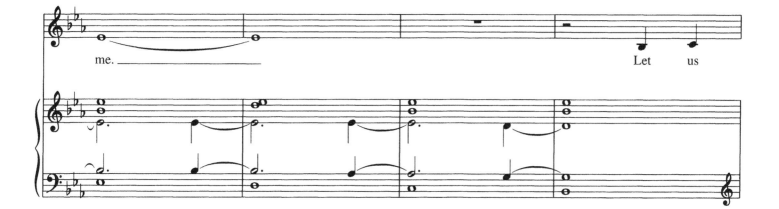

me. _____ Let us

drink wine to - geth-er on our knees, _____ Let us

drink wine to - geth-er on our knees. _____ When I

cresc. poco

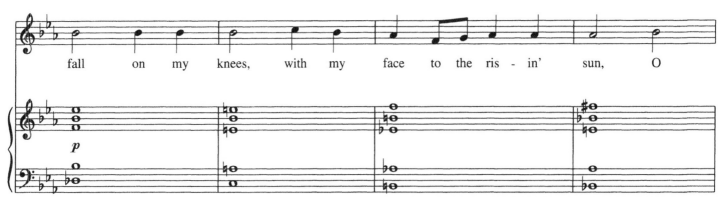

fall on my knees, with my face to the ris - in' sun, O

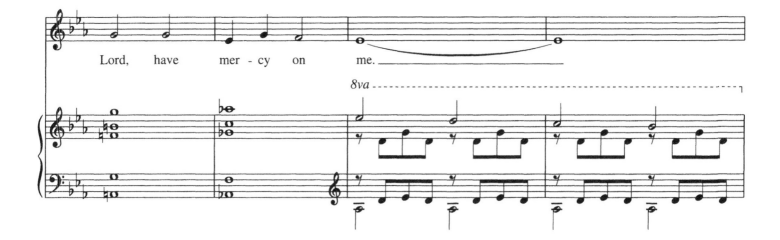

Lord, have mer - cy on me.

Let us praise God to -

geth - er on our knees, Let us praise God to -

(either R.H. or L.H.)

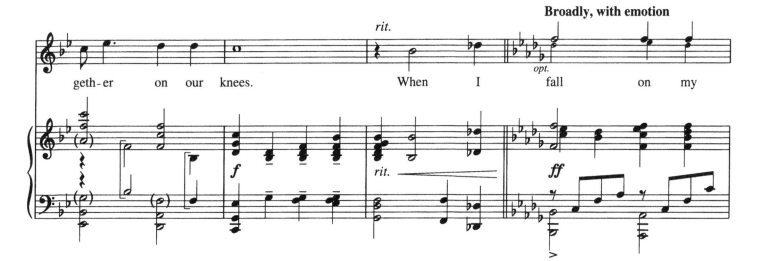

geth-er on our knees. When I fall on my

knees, with my face to the ris-in' sun, ___

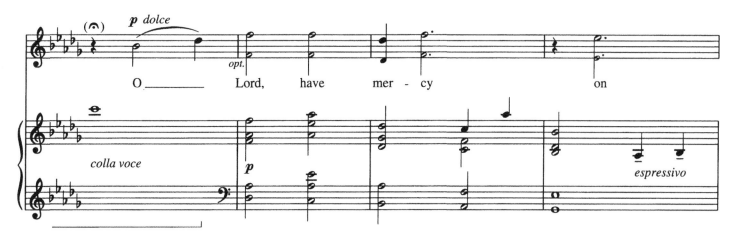

O ___ Lord, have mer-cy on

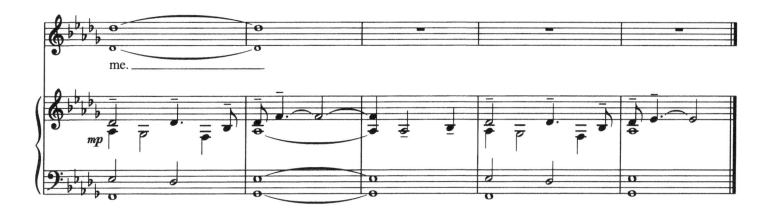

me. ___

for Reed and Terri

THIS IS MY FATHER'S WORLD

Maltbie D. Babcock, 1901

traditional English melody
first adapted by Franklin L. Sheppard, 1915
arranged by Richard Walters

This is my Fa - ther's world; I ___

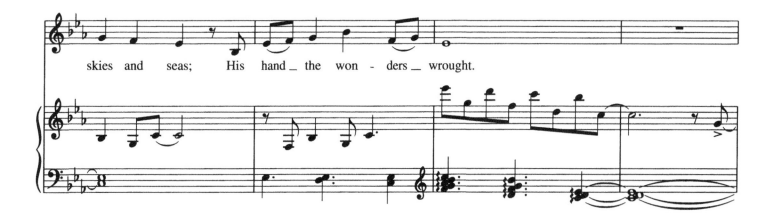

rest me in the thought of rocks and trees, of ___

skies and seas; His hand _ the won - ders _ wrought.

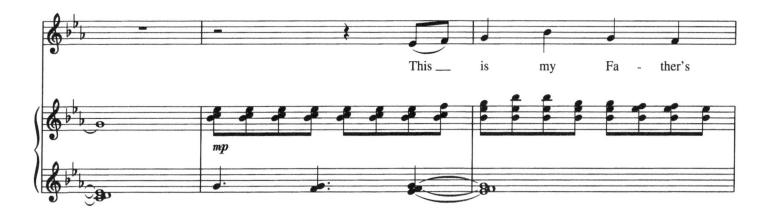

This ___ is my Fa - ther's

world; The birds their car - ols raise; The

morn - ing light, the lil - y white, De - clare their mak - er's

praise. This is my Fa - ther's world; He

shines in all that's fair. In the rust - ling grass I hear him pass; He

speaks_ to me ev-'ry-where.

cresc. mf

A little slower
poco rit.

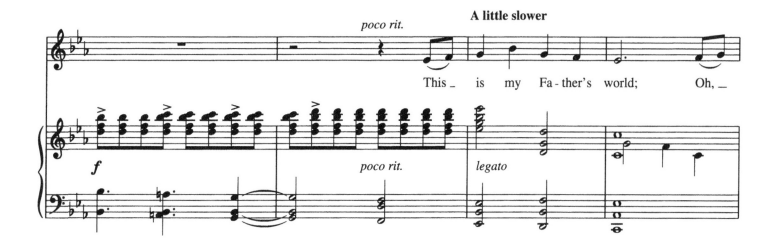

This _ is my Fa-ther's world; Oh, _

f poco rit. legato

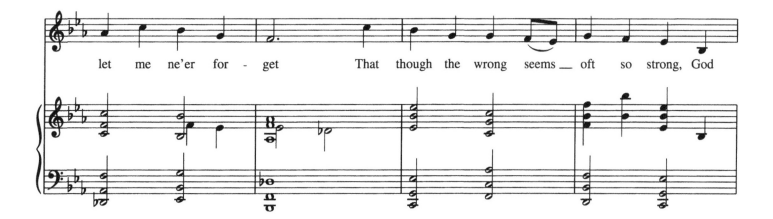

let me ne'er for - get That though the wrong seems _ oft so strong, God

is _ the ru - ler _ yet. This is my Fa-ther's world, Why _

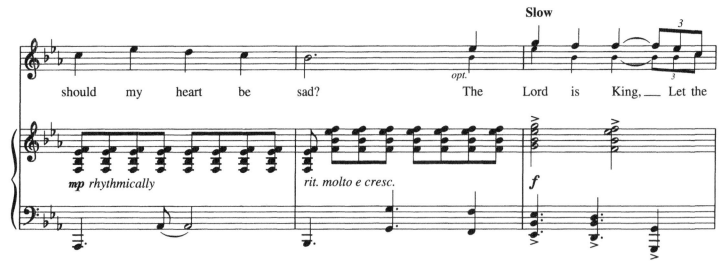

should my heart be sad? *opt.* The Lord is King, __ Let the

mp rhythmically   *rit. molto e cresc.*   *f*

Slow

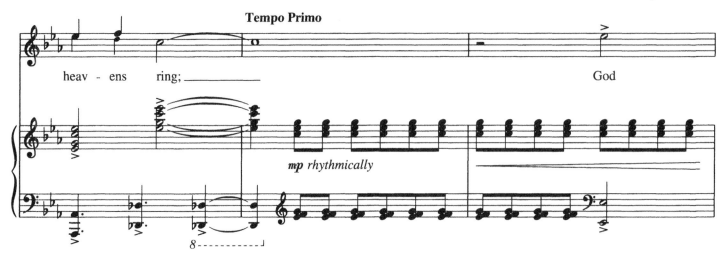

heav - ens ring; _____ God

mp rhythmically

Tempo Primo

reigns, let the earth be glad. _____

f

(non rit.)

for Paul and Lou

WONDROUS LOVE

American Folk Hymn
arranged by Richard Walters

Slow, steady

p

Medium Voice:

What won - drous love is this, O my soul, O my

soul, What won - drous love is this. O my

sim.

High Voice joins (unison):

soul. What won - drous love is this that caused the Lord of

lay a - side His crown for my soul, for my soul, He

soul, _____ O my

lay a - side His crown for my soul.

soul. _____

legato

mp

mp

High Voice:

Medium Voice:

won - drous love is this, O my soul, O my

soul, What won - drous love is this, O my

What won - drous love is

this, O my soul O my soul, What

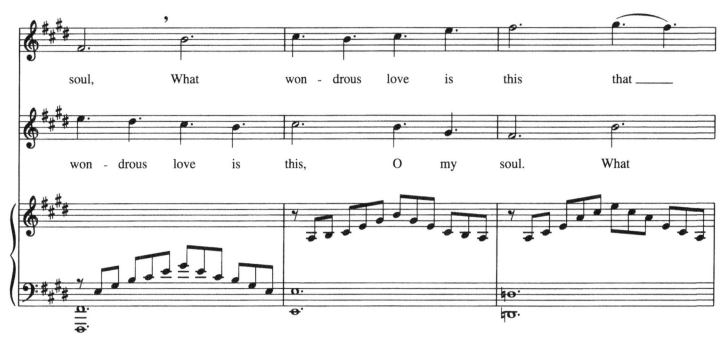

soul, What won - drous love is this that _____

won - drous love is this, O my soul. What

caused the Lord _ of bliss to bear the dread - ful

won - drous love is this that caused the Lord _ of

curse for my soul, for my soul, to

bliss to bear the dread - ful curse for my

for Carol and Anne

ALL CREATURES OF OUR GOD AND KING

after Psalm 148
Francis of Assisi, c. 1225
translated by William Draper (alt.)

"Lasst uns Erfreuen"
melody from
Geistliche Kirchengesäng, Cologne 1623
adapted by Ralph Vaughan Williams, 1906
arranged by Richard Walters

Moderato, stately

Medium voice:

All crea-tures of our God and

King, _____ Lift up your voice and with us sing _____

_____ Al-le-lu-ia, Al-le-lu-ia! _____ Thou

burn-ing sun with gold-en beam, _____ Thou sil - ver moon with soft - er

gleam, _____ O ___ praise Him, O ___ praise Him, ___

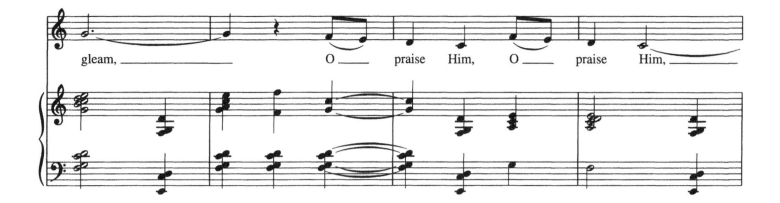

Al - le - lu - ia, Al - le - lu - ia, Al - le -

Allegretto   **High voice:**

lu - ia! _____   Thou

mp rhythmically   *sim.*

rush-ing wind that are so strong, _____ Ye clouds that sail in heav'n a -

long, _____ O _ praise Him, Al - le - lu - ia! _____

_____ Thou ris - ing morn, in praise re - joice, _____ Ye

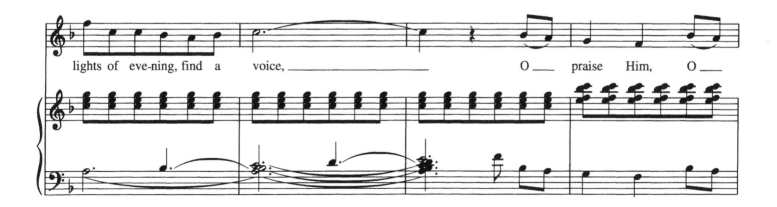

lights of eve-ning, find a voice, _____ O _ praise Him, O _____

praise Him, _____ Al - le - lu - ia, Al - le -

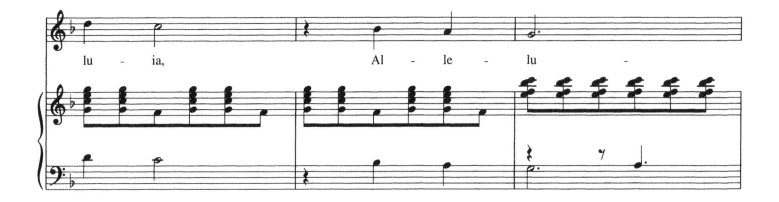

lu - ia, Al - le - lu -

ia! _____

Thou flow-ing wa-ter, pure and clear,_____ Make

Thou flow-ing wa-ter, pure and clear,_____

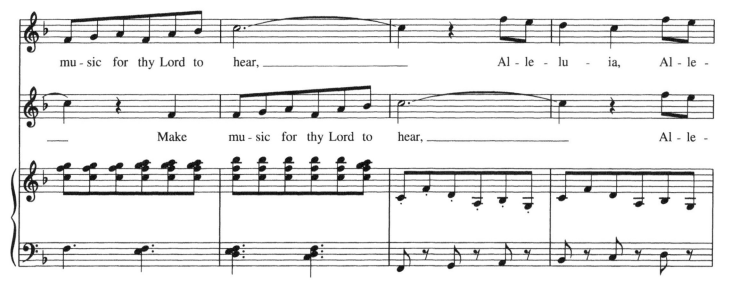

mu-sic for thy Lord to hear,_____ Al-le-lu-ia, Al-le-

Make mu-sic for thy Lord to hear,_____ Al-le-

lu-ia!_____ Thou fire so mas-ter-ful and bright, That

lu-ia, Al-le-lu-ia!_____ Thou fire so mas-ter-ful and

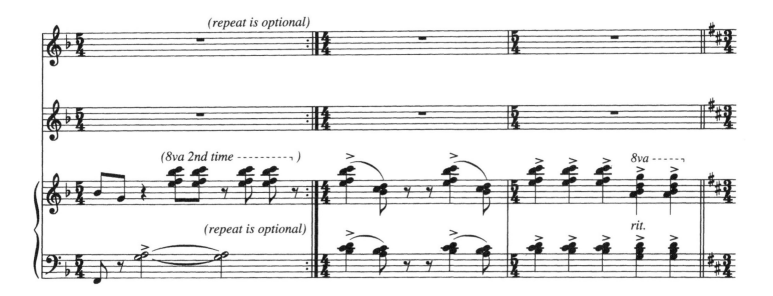

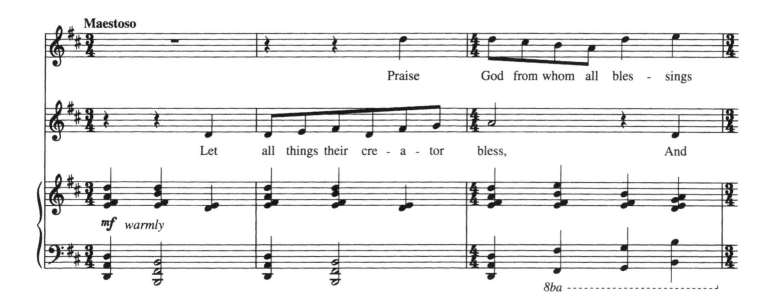

flow, Praise Him, all crea-tures here be - low;

wor - ship him in hum-ble - ness, O____ praise Him, Al - le -

8ba-----

Praise Him a - bove, ye heav'n - ly host,____ Praise

lu - ia! Praise, praise the Fa - ther, praise the

8ba----- *8ba-----*

Fa - ther, Son and Ho - ly Ghost.____

Son, And praise the Spi - rit, Three in One.____

(8)-----

Al - le - lu,   Al - le - lu - ia!

lu,   Al - le - lu,   Al - le - lu - ia!

a tempo

8va

R.H.

a tempo

8ba

f

8ba

8ba